THE INDIAN OCEAN

EVERGREEN is an imprint of Benedikt Taschen Verlag GmbH

© for this edition: 1998 Benedikt Taschen Verlag GmbH
Hohenzollernring 53, D–50672 Köln
© 1997 Editions du Chêne – Hachette Livre – L'Océan indien
Under the direction of Michel Buntz – Hoa Qui Photographic Agency
Editor: Corinne Fossey
Maps and illustrations: Jean-Michel Kirsch
Text: Eliane Georges
Photographs: Christian Vaisse
Cover: Angelika Taschen, Cologne
Translated by Simon Knight
In association with First Edition Translations Ltd, Cambridge
Realization of the English edition by First Edition Translations Ltd, Cambridge

Printed in Italy
ISBN 3-8228-7756-5

THE INDIAN OCEAN

MADAGASCAR RÉUNION MAURITIUS THE SEYCHELLES

Text ELIANE GEORGES
Photographs CHRISTIAN VAISSE

EVERGREEN

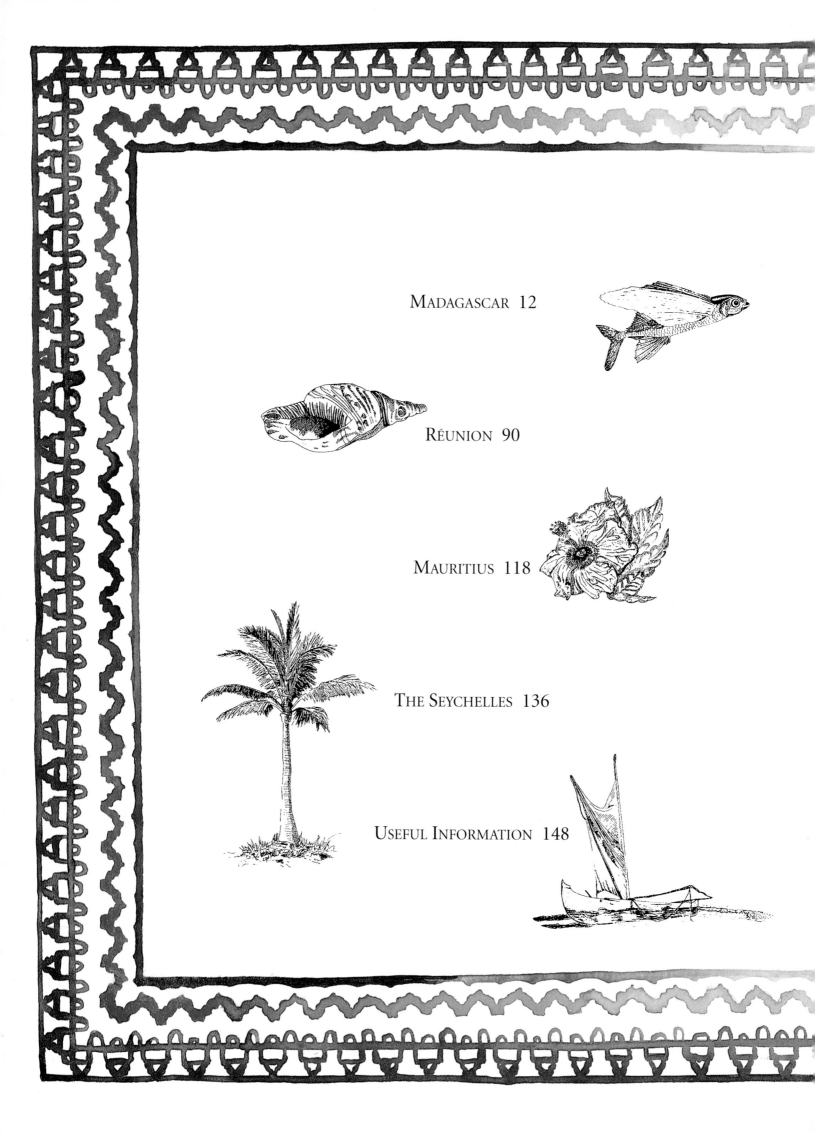

THE SEYCHELLES

COMORES

Moroni

CAP
D'AMBRE

Mayotte

Antsiranana

Vohimarina

Nosy-Be

Sambava

Antalaha

Mahajanga

Sofia

Mitsinjo

CAP
MASOALA

Ambodifototra

Mahavelona

Toamasina

MADAGASCAR

Antananarivo

Antsirabe

Mahanoro

MAURITIUS

Morondava

Ambositra

Mananjary

Fianavantsoa

Canal de Pangalanes

Manakara

RÉUNION

Farafangana

Toliary

Ambovombe

CAP
SAINTE MARIE

The plane vibrates as it approaches Bird Island. Beneath its sun-splashed wings, the tiny speck of land looks like an oyster set in the glassy waters of its lagoon.

The moment you are out of the plane, a wave of sultry heat rises from the tarmac – here, it is only four degrees south of the Equator – but in July a gentle southwest breeze is blowing: the sœte, a dry monsoon wind. Bird Island is one of the smaller of the Seychelles, one and a half kilometres (one mile) long, 800 metres (2,625 ft) wide, a speck in the ocean, covered with guano. You can walk round it in an hour and a half, barefoot in the soft sand, avoiding the driftwood.

The only accommodation is a lodge where you can spend the night: bungalows with white mosquito nets scattered among frangipani trees imported onto the coral reef.

As you walk along the beach, you hear a constant rumbling, like a waterfall, caused by the ocean swell breaking over the distant banks of coral. Then, gradually, you become aware of a strange confabulation, interspersed with strident voices. At first, it consists merely of mocking cries, rustling like silk, as birds glide overhead, white underparts standing out against the blue sky. But why do they brush against you like that, flying in slow motion, half threatening? Then, as you progress along the sand, among veloutiers and other low-growing bushes, towards the centre of the island, the sound becomes deafening. And suddenly, there it is before you, nightmarish as a scene from a Hitchcock film: on the bare, sandy ground, millions of black-and-white sooty terns are sitting on their eggs, amid a constant flapping of wings and furious screeching. Their numbers are such that, in the distance, above the feathery casuarina trees, the sky is virtually blotted out. You would think that a biblical plague, worse than the grasshoppers of Egypt, was descending on the world.

Of course, there is also the Indian Ocean you see on postcards: Blue Bay, on Mauritius, its waters a velvety, deep ultramarine; Anse Lazio, on Praslin, tacamaque trees laid over by the trade winds shading its sun-drenched beach; the long foam-topped rollers of Saint Gilles, on the island of Réunion, bearing surfers towards the shore; the transparent, pale turquoise lagoon of the Anse d'Argent on La Digue, when the sky is so intense you would think it was polarized. This is the time to share in the idleness of the gods, feet spread in the volcanic sand, snorkel permanently grasped between the teeth, in warm, living waters patrolled by brilliantly coloured fish. Sergeant majors, damselfish, royal angel fish, purple cardinals and marbled hamlets swim past, as in an enchanted tropical aquarium, from which you eventually emerge with flippered feet, skin encrusted with salt, intoxicated by the immensity of ocean. Voluptuous tropics! The heat enfolds you in its embrace, and the island indolence is expressed to perfection in the Creole language, a laid-back, lisping mode of speech which, to quote the locals, "cuts across words, because it grows in an easy-going land".

But leave the lagoon; move out into the ocean. There is a powerful swell. Suddenly, the beach drops away steeply into hidden depths. The violent waters have drowned the original wound. A hundred and sixty million years ago, Africa and Asia were still one, joined by the immense continent of Gondwanaland. For reasons best known to itself, it sank beneath the deep blue waters of the Indian Ocean. All that is left is Madagascar, the great red island, drifting like a long laterite liner off the African coast, with its green paddy fields, grey elephant-skinned baobabs, prehistoric chameleons, strange lemurs and ancient kings with interminable names, like the seventh ruler of Imerina: Andriantsimitoviaminandriandehibe. An archaic Noah's ark, until recently navigating under the red flag of socialism. Then there are the fragile, scattered flotillas of the Seychelles, the Comoro Islands and the Maldives. And the more solitary vessels of Réunion, Mauritius and Rodrigues, lost in the ocean. Conscious of their splendid isolation in the vastness of the sea, the people of Réunion have a pithy expression: "Alors! vous la saute la mer?" (So, you are jumping the sea?), they say to those who are venturing abroad. The visitor cannot but notice the solitude of these island peoples.

And yet… sniff again the pungency of the ocean breeze. Let your gaze extend far out to the watery horizon. Sunken galleons, gold, ivory, cargoes of cardamom and precious stones, ebony and costly silks, the sweat of slaves, missionary fervour, ambitious dreams of piracy – what passions have stirred these deep waters!

Lying athwart the great maritime spice routes, object of greed and treachery, the islands of the Indian Ocean exhale a heady perfume of battles long ago. Arabs, Portuguese, Dutch, British and French all planted their flags on these shores. Africans, Indonesians, Indians and Chinese came to settle and trade. The great powers confronted one another under the sardonic gaze of gentlemen of fortune, buccaneers who ruthlessly scoured the seas. Hence, these peoples who love to celebrate, in whose veins runs the blood of so many different races.

Although the islands no longer march to an epic strain, they still have to cope with the cyclones which, from November to April, roam the Indian Ocean. A coppery evening sky, and you will see the islanders eaten up with anxiety. As soon as the radio announces that one is on its way, there is a furious bustle of preparation. Everywhere you hear the sound of hammers, nailing lengths of timber across rickety doors. Houses big and small must dance to the wind's tune, resonating like a ship's hull in a heavy swell. One year, the cyclones were so frequent that, in giving each a woman's name, they ran right through the alphabet. And all the islands bear their scars.

Yet it is one of the miracles of the tropics that life begins again with renewed vitality. Though flayed alive, the flame trees draw up fresh sap and break out into flower. The ramparts of the cirques – Réunion's great natural amphitheatres – are clothed with a profusion of white blossom. And again, the voluptuous fragrance of vanilla and ylang-ylang wafts down the streets like syrup.

It is the smells that linger when you leave the Indian Ocean. Maybe you carry away just a tiny geranium leaf, all scratched and torn, surreptitiously pinched from the copper still. Lying in the moist palm of your hand, it gives off its intoxicating aroma of rose and pepper…

*At Morondava,
on the west coast,
the men set off to fish
in deep water, while the
womenfolk use mosquito
netting to catch a delicious
meal of small fry.*

They call it the "Island of Perfumes", so intoxicating is the fragrance of ylang-ylang, vanilla, pepper and other spices. Its waters are of a disconcerting clarity; its sky a flawless blue. Sea always warm, sand a dazzling white, villages of native huts nestling in groves of coconut palms: the island of Nosy Be, lying fifteen or so kilometres (ten miles) off the northwest coast of Madagascar, could be taken for a fragment of Polynesia adrift in the Indian Ocean. Beginning with this tiny volcanic Eden is the lazy way to approach the great enigmatic island of Madagascar. Like the outrigger canoes returning in the evening from a day's fishing, life flows *mora mora*, gently, without hurry. The sun pours a honeyed light over the sugarcane fields, creating a sense of voluptuousness and languor: Nosy Be is a place you could stay and lose track of time.

Appropriately, the Malagasy tourist authorities have named this part of northwest Madagascar "the coast of unexplored islands". The enchanting off-shore archipelago includes Nosy Tanikely, with its sparkling coral reef; Nosy Komba, home of the Black lemur (*L. macaco*); Nosy Sakatia, where the fruit bats roost; Nosy Iranja and

Nosy Mitsio, unspoilt, turtle-haunted islets – jewels of Madagascar's
5,000-kilometre (3,100-mile) coastline.

Five thousand kilometres! It is difficult to grasp. Fourth largest
island in the world by area, Madagascar stretches north–south off
the southeast coast of Africa, its western flank bathed by the
Mozambique Channel, its eastern shores facing the immensity of
the Indian Ocean. The moment you penetrate into the hinterland,
into the depths of luxuriant virgin forests or the weird vegetation
of vast denuded plateaux, Madagascar's long interface with the surrounding ocean is quickly forgotten. Yet, this island-continent owes
everything to the sea: Madagascar's history begins with an outrigger canoe. According to Louis des Garniers, it was giant outrigger
canoes which, "borne by winds and currents, brought the ancestors
of the present-day Malagasy across the ocean, probably in the early
centuries of the Christian era".

The African ancestry is obvious: Africa is not far away. As for the
contribution made by Malayo-Polynesian peoples, who are thought
to have originated in southern China over 10,000 years ago, and

*I*ndonesian in origin, the outrigger
canoe is a reminder of the long voyage
made by the ancestors of the
Malagasy.

came via Indonesia, it can be detected in the language, in agricultural techniques and, above all, in facial features, which betray an Asiatic gentleness.

It is now accepted that Neolithic navigators could have undertaken such a voyage across the Indian Ocean, defying storm and hunger. If proof there had to be, it was given on 6 August 1985, when Bob Hobman and his crew, sailing an outrigger canoe of the kind used in prehistoric times, completed an amazing crossing. Their primitive craft, the *Sarimanok*, was the hollowed-out trunk of a huge giho tree, with plaited-bark rigging and sails woven from plant fibres. They left Indonesia and sailed by dead reckoning for 63 days, until the cliffs of Cap d'Ambre, in the extreme north of Madagascar, at last loomed up before them. Unable to find the narrow channel through the reef before nightfall, they were taken in tow to Mayotte, in the Comoro Islands. But the point was made: by completing the voyage from Indonesia to Madagascar, they had demonstrated that the island could well have been settled by peoples from the Malayo-Polynesian region. And the *Sarimanok*, now in dry dock on the

*O*n the harbour-side in Hellville, *Nosy Be, local craftsmen sell models of west-coast dhows (*botry*) and fine examples of* resselé *(Richelieu) embroidery.*

*A*ppearance-conscious Malagasy girls adorn themselves for a dance to celebrate the rice harvest.

island of Nosy Be, remains as silent witness to their daring exploit. Irregular waves of migration continued until the thirteenth century. The *Book of Wonders of India* tells how, between the ninth and tenth centuries, a thousand wak-wak canoes were sighted in the Mozambique Channel, "wak-wak" being the Arab term for the Indonesians. If we then add a third source of immigration, Persians from Chiraz and Arabs who spread southwards down the African coast and reached Madagascar via the Comoros, we see how the island became such a human jigsaw puzzle, settled by eighteen officially recognized ethnic groups.

Such are the origins of the Sakalava, "people of the long valleys"; Merina, "people of the heights"; Antandroy, "people who live among the thorns"; Antaimoro, "people who live on the banks"; Betsimisaraka, "the many who do not separate"; and the various

*M*any festivities are held to
celebrate the rice harvest, an
opportunity for these
young Sakalava girls to
make up in the traditional way.

other groups. For centuries, they lived in small, self-contained kingdoms, their ways and customs preserved by the island's strange topology: wide rivers, long mountain chains, and the thick forests that have since been destroyed.

This settlement, which for historian Hubert Deschamps remains "the world's most fascinating enigma", is still shrouded in mystery, despite the best efforts of contemporary research. Why, for instance, when the Malagasy transplant their young rice plants after the Indonesian fashion, does the vocabulary used for rice cultivation derive from the Dravidian languages of southern India?

And their facial features – reflecting this blending of cultures at the meeting point of two continents – are disorientating. A group of women walk along the road shaded by tall, leafy breadfruit trees. As you glance from one to another, you are aware of subtle combinations: the dusky complexion of the Abyssinian, the slanting eyes of the Asiatic, the features of Semite and Bantu, sometimes even the slightly flat-nosed softness of the Polynesian. The Malagasy have the smiling appearance of Africans, but without their exuberance,

moderated by the enigmatic expression of the Oriental. Their eyes focus on the horizon, as if they were watching for some hidden presence lurking in the depths of earth and sky. And they will answer your questions in a gentle murmur, *mora mora*, in a tone suggestive of doubt and scepticism.

Mysticism is perhaps the word. Here, the living keep faith with the dead. Eleven million Malagasy is a meaningless statistic, when the ancestors are ever present. "They are like salt, which may dissolve in water, but does not disappear." The razana, omnipotent ancestors, are invoked every single day, regaled with sweet offerings of honey, fruits and flowers, honoured with the blood of hump-backed zebu cattle on special feast days. And then, there are the many *fady*, taboos instituted by the ancestors, which regulate daily life, and whose solemn observance goes far to explain the impenetrable Malagasy reserve.

In the midst of daily life, the unseen constantly breaks surface. Rumours – *tsaho* – run riot, mixing truth and falsehood, as in a waking dream. "Last night, a star began spinning in the sky. A

Women setting off to fish for small fry. The fish are caught in baskets and transferred to the small baskets they carry on their heads.

The mangrove swamps of the west coast are the domain of crabs and shrimps and of a wealth of bird species, such as teal, knob-billed duck, ibis and pink flamingo.

creature, half man, half horse, appeared on the beach." And often the *mpisikidy*, a kind of diviner or witch doctor, has to be consulted. Malagasy history is strongly marked by this belief in the supernatural. In the nineteenth century, Ranavalona I, all-powerful queen of the central highlands, would appear in public dressed in the sumptuous silk and brocade creations of French couturiers. But Antananarivo, her capital, "city of a thousand warriors", was a forbidden city, defended like a tomb. None could come through its heavy granite gateway without the permission of the *mpisikidy*, interpreter of oracles. Sovereign by divine right, fiercely nationalistic, this bloody tyrant dispensed justice by ordeal. Suspects were made to undergo trial by poison, presumed guilty unless they survived. Foreign conspirators, such as the Austrian adventuress Ida Pfeiffer, who hatched a plot to dethrone her, barely escaped the same treatment.

Her more liberal and tolerant son, Radama II, decided to introduce reforms and throw the island open to foreign investors. The reactionary faction at court was not pleased, and ministers fomented a

coup d'état. In the surrounding villages, men fell into a trance, claiming to speak in the name of the late queen, the terrible Ranavalona, furious at seeing her kingdom weakened in this way. They formed a procession, bearing an empty chair in which she was said to preside. Possessed by the forces of evil, these men aroused feelings of awe. When they arrived at the royal palace, in Antananarivo, King Radama, too, was seized with mortal dread. Who was seated there, in the empty chair, but the ghost of his mother, returned from the place of darkness to call him to account? Paralyzed by fear, he allowed himself to be strangled by army officers.

Madagascar has not been immune to European greed. Over five centuries, by force of arms and religious influence, the Portuguese, British and French attempted to bend the island to their will. But the Malagasy soul is not so easy to subject. What remains today of the 60-odd years of French colonization? Not a great deal, apart from the French language, widely spoken and understood. It serves as a second language, after the Merina tongue of the central highlands, which is regarded as the national language, over and above

The principal rivers of the west coast, such as the Betsiboka, Mahajamba and Mahavavy, form great deltas. As a result of bush fires, no plant cover is left to protect the fertile soil upstream.

the many dialect variants. In the architecture of certain coastal towns, one may nevertheless sense a nostalgia for a colourful past. In the extreme north, perched on a promontory, Antsiranana (formerly Diego-Suarez) has the charm of an old colonial town of fading splendour. The crescent moons engraved on the arcades of its fine Indian houses are evidence of a strong Islamic influence. Farther down the west coast, Mahajanga (formerly Majunga), ancient capital of the Sakalava kingdom, occupies a headland between the sea and the red, silt-laden waters of the Betsiboka Estuary. A crossroads of trade between Africa, Arabia and Asia, this town, too, has had a tumultuous history. But now, the dhows and coolies have departed. Its port is dying. The mangrove swamps are taking over. In the rainy season, the dirt roads leaving the Betsiboka delta often become impassable. The rampant forests of mangrove trees are a refuge for the last crocodiles. At dawn, when all is still locked in sleep, they can be seen crossing the road, moving from one area of marshland to the next, often bearing a clump of reeds or some other aquatic plant.

Sugar-cane in flower. One of Madagascar's four sugar refineries is at Djamandjary, in Nosy Be, which produces an excellent rum.

The Betsileo of the southern highland region are hard-working farmers, who struggle to make a living in this difficult terrain. Their kipahy, or terraced rice fields, give good yields.

The central highlands of Madagascar, pushed up by the mountain ranges that form the island's backbone, rise to an average altitude of 1,000 metres (3,280 ft). The so-called "Hauts Plateaux" are a land of rice, wind and ancestral spirits. From the coast, they can be reached by *taxi-brousse* (bush taxi), the universal means of local transport. Stuffed solid with passengers, roof-rack overflowing with crates of foodstuffs and strong-smelling sacks sewn up with string, the heroic vehicle struggles up towards the Merina or Betsileo country over roads pock-marked with puddles and pot-holes, climbing through hills terraced with paddy fields. Open to the overarching sky, the highlands run from north to south, divided up by gentler valleys, softened by the hand of man. Here in the central highlands occurred the great events of Malagasy history, after the arrival of the final waves of Indonesian settlers. By dint of endless struggles with unsubdued tribes, their descendants eventually formed an influential caste ruling over a land known as Imerina, a confederation of pocket-sized, turbulent kingdoms. Having become sovereign of the stronghold of Ambohimanga in

*T*erraced rice fields are a feature of the central highlands of Madagascar,
at an average altitude of 1,000 m (3,280 ft).

• The zebu •

The zebu – *omby* in Malagasy – is a national institution, as important in the popular mind as rice. Ten million of these odd-looking beasts are said to roam the bushlands of Madagascar, their ears marked with the family symbol as proof of ownership. Farmers also use them for treading the mud in the flooded paddy fields, an activity in which the whole family is involved. Though excellent, not much Malagasy meat is exported, as slaughterhouses do not meet the required health and safety standards. But the zebu is so highly prized among the Malagasy, they are not really concerned about its monetary value. The herd takes part in all the village ceremonies, lowing at funerals to help the human participants call up the spirits of the ancestors. And when a zebu is sacrificed, to atone for a sin or have its skull set up on the owner's tomb, the village diviner can be counted on to interpret its behaviour.

The red, mud-brick houses around Antananarivo often have gables like those of the Creole houses in Réunion or Mauritius.

1787, Andrianampoinimerina ("lord in the heart of Imerina") set out to "make Imerina a single-coloured guinea-fowl". A clever strategist, he married one woman from each of the noble families ruling over the 12 sacred hills of Imerina. After subjugating the king of Antananarivo, he managed to extend his hegemony to the whole of the highlands, making vassals of the Betsileo and Sihanaka peoples. The architect of Malagasy unity, this astute monarch also introduced an ambitious economic policy. He understood the importance of rice, the staple food of the Malagasy, and let it be known that the bond between king and paddy field was indissoluble. Although he had never seen the ocean, on his death, in 1810, he bequeathed to his son, Radama, this astonishing saying, by way of political testament: "The sea will be the limit of my paddy field". Harsh and windswept, this region of Imerina, its climate tempered by altitude, is nevertheless one of the most fertile parts of Madagascar. The prevailing mood is one of muted melancholy. The grey-green of the bare, rounded hills and valleys, and the more vivid splashes of the young rice plants, standing in water-filled

nursery beds, give the landscape an Asiatic fluidity. But here, too, the land is bleeding. And the mud-brick villages, their walls daubed with a red wash, seem bathed in blood. Blown by the restless wind, even the horns of the humpbacked cattle are caked in a fine, red, lateritic dust. Just add the white of the decorticated rice, and you have the flag of the "Repoblika Malagasy": red, green and white. Rice – *vary* – is still the staff of life. The most popular dish is *romazava*: rice and lumps of beef, soaked with a clear broth containing pieces of tomato and the leaves and flowers of *brèdes mafana*, a hot, fragrant Malagasy herb. It is washed down with *ranovola*, water boiled in the pot with the burnt scrapings of the rice, which is surprisingly refreshing and safe to drink.

Intelligent and hard-working, the peasant farmers of Imerina busy themselves discreetly about their daily tasks. But they have always to struggle against the hazards of the climate, particularly the heavy rains of the warm season, which flood the rice-growing areas from December to March. Erosion is a constant problem, washing away the fragile layer of lateritic soil and forming a hard, red crust. In

After the rice harvest, the paddy is put out to dry on large mats.

• "Turning the dead" •

Each year, during July and August, musicians congregate in the villages of the Malagasy highlands to celebrate *famadihana*, a ceremony during which the dead are exhumed and fêted, then reburied. This is the most spectacular manifestation of the cult of the ancestors. Usually, one of the departed will have appeared in a dream to complain of neglect, in which case the village astrologer is consulted to fix a propitious day. Or it could be that a person who has died far from home needs to be brought back to the family tomb. The family will then invite guests to partake of a great feast, with musicians (*mpihiragasy*) in attendance. Large quantities of illicit alcohol, known as *betsa-betsa*, are drunk, putting the "mourners" in the mood to dance. Amid merry jubilation, the tomb is opened, the mummified body removed and carried at head height. Later, the corpse is wrapped in a new silk shroud, or *lambamena*. Finally, after seven circuits of the tomb, it is returned to its resting place.

Mpihiragasy, *groups of dancers and musicians, travel from village to village to play at the* famadihana *ceremonies, when the dead are exhumed and fêted during the dry Malagasy "winter".*

order to control better the devastating flooding of the Ikopa, Sisaony and Mamba rivers, back in the eighteenth century King Andrianampoinimerina built an impressive network of irrigation channels and dams. It still waters the vast Betsimitatatra Plain, around Antananarivo, the city's all-important granary. In the rays of the setting sun, it glistens in the distance like a mirror broken into a thousand fragments, a blue stained-glass window whose leaded strips are trod, ant-like, by the women returning from pricking out the young rice plants. Further south, in the region of Fianarantsoa, the Betsileo are reckoned to be the most skilled rice-growers in all Madagascar. Robust, diligent people, they cultivate their crops on irrigated terraces, as in Bali or the Philippines. And they have preserved other rites and customs inherited from their Indonesian ancestors. As well as the dominant Merina and Betsileo, other ethnic groups of the Malagasy highlands are the Sihanaka ("the people who live near the lake"), around Lake Alaotra, who are specialists in irrigated rice-growing; the Bezanozano ("the people with many plaits"), and the Tanala ("people of the forest").

*Mauve is the colour of
Antananarivo in October,
when the jacarandas around
Lake Anosy come into flower.*

Antananarivo – formerly Tananarive, but known colloquially as Tana – clings to its 12 hills. Steep, narrow streets sunk in places after the rains, ochre façades flaming in the evening sun, wooden balconies tottering against brick and concrete-built houses, the city has grown quickly, chaotic and capricious, hugging the terrain, watched over by the austere mass of the Lycée Gallieni.

Licked by the groundswell of paddy fields which come to rest at its feet, Madagascar's capital is a mountain city, by turns parochial and tumultuous, pungent and provocative as hot spice. Its districts are like separate villages, each with its own market and ox-drawn carts. And you can easily get lost in its labyrinth of lanes and endless stairways, which leave you breathless as you climb up one hill and down another.

Situated in the heart of the Hauts Plateaux, in the old Merina (pronounced "merne") kingdom, in a predominantly agricultural region, the city is reminiscent of a medieval court of miracles. With closed expressions, black hair, prominent cheekbones, the Merina peasant folk rub shoulders with local dignitaries, wealthy traders

and privileged *vazaha* (foreigners). But the growing number of *quatr'amis*, professional beggars who lie in wait at the entrance to the big hotels, is eloquent testimony to the economic deprivation suffered by much of the population.

You absolutely must arrange to be in Tana for the *Zoma*, the great Friday market, life and soul of the lower town. Already on Thursday evening, stallholders begin flowing in from the surrounding area, ready to spend a night in the open if it means getting a good position among the forest of white parasols. The Avenue de l'Indépendence, where in the 1930s French settlers would congregate on café terraces to discuss the affairs of the metropole, is soon a tight mass of people. But everything takes place in such amazing silence. According to Florence Théard, the reason this great market is never the scene of shouting, arguments or laughter is that a royal shroud of reserve, a mixture of melancholy and dignity, wraps the shoulders of the highland Merina people, like the white *lamba* worn by their womenfolk. Yet, beneath the apparent chaos, the Zoma is highly organized. Absolutely everything is on sale: nails sold by weight,

*L*ake Anosy was once a lake of sweet water, where the annual Fandroana, or bathing, ceremony – a purification ritual involving the queen – was held.

Unusually for a developing country, the upper town of Antananarivo has retained its traditional style of architecture.

string by the metre, vanilla pods or the most sublime orchids. But each corporation has its own area: foodstuffs in the central part, ironmongery in the brick pavilions, second-hand items and bric-à-brac on the stairways on the east side of the market place, itinerant opticians and rubber-stamp makers on the flights of steps opposite. Some craftsmen have had the presence of mind to design local-style suitcases, made from hammered-out old tin cans, in which you can pack your purchases.

In the upper town is the site of the Queen's Palace, or more accurately a complex of royal buildings, erected during the various reigns of the Merina dynasty. Sadly, they were gutted by fire in November 1996. Only the stone-built, outer shell of the main palace remains. Clad in costly hardwoods and adorned with glassware, the smaller pavilions betrayed the court's fondness for pomp and circumstance. The site is reached by a road overlooking a ravine, with cannons from the days when the *rova*, or royal compound, still needed to be defended from attack. From the nearby cliff of Ampamarinana, or "place of hurling", Christians persecuted during the time of

Ranavalona I, in 1849, were thrown to their deaths on the rocks below. You can also see the house of Jean Laborde. Born at Auch, in the Pyrenean foothills, in 1806, this dashing young cavalry officer was wrecked on the coast of Madagascar on the return voyage from India. When presented to the queen, he won her confidence and went on to set up a full-scale industrial complex, which he called Soatsimanampiovana, literally "the beauty that does not change". As well as the guns and powder commissioned by Ranavalona, his workshops turned out lightning conductors, bricks, tiles, soap, earthenware and pottery. A brilliant jack of all trades, Jean Laborde also acclimatized fruit trees, Normandy cattle and sheep from Egypt, and laid out a zoological garden. A perfect gentleman, he even introduced the waltz to the ladies of the court. He was the architect of the main palace, built for Ranavalona I in 1839. Before the recent fire, it was supported by a single wooden pillar, 39 metres (128 ft) high. Legend has it that two thousand of the ten thousand slaves employed in transporting this huge tree trunk from the forests of the east coast perished along the way.

All the produce of Madagascar is to be found under the white parasols of the great Friday market, or Zoma.

*O*n Fridays, Antananarivo's main
square is the scene of intense
economic activity. Broom sellers set
out their wares beside the makers of
angady – *spades used for turning the
clods in the paddy fields.*

*A*t Barenty, near Amboasary, sisal
is the crop best suited to the drought
conditions of the Malagasy south.
The fibres are washed and dried in
the sun before being carded by the
women. Sisal is an export product.

The Pangalanes Canal, running parallel with the east coast, has recently been restored to encourage water-borne traffic.

From Tana, the train – one of the more tangible reminders of the 60 years of French colonization – grinds its way in a metallic clatter of protesting axles and rattling wheels towards Toamasina ("it seems salty"), formerly Tamatave, the great port of Madagascar's east coast.

Twelve hours to cover 370 kilometres (230 miles), with nearly 40 stops on the way, but what a journey! Having crossed the rice-growing plains of the highlands, the locomotive begins its descent, tackling an escarpment clothed in creepers and cascades of greenery, with occasional glimpses of sun-lit valleys closed in by mountains. Soon the atmosphere becomes heavier and more humid, and it is time to switch on the fan. Halfway, the train stops at Perinet (Andasibe), whose nature reserve shelters rare orchids and the largest of Madagascar's lemurs, the indri or babakoto (*Indri indri*), with its eerie, wailing cry. The dense primary forest in this area is under threat. Every day, slash-and-burn agriculture (*tavy*) destroys a little more of the remaining virgin forest, and a secondary growth of pandanus, ravenala (traveller's tree), bamboo and eucalyptus

takes over from the original hardwood species. As it crosses the
banana plantations of the coastal strip, the train begins a crazy
pitching motion: land crabs have undermined the tracks and the
rails have become deformed. The soft breath of the *alizé* (trade
wind) wafts through the window.

*B*amboo rafts are still made around
Toamasina on the east coast.

The east coast, with its scent of cinnamon, shark-infested waters
and memories of piracy, has a hot, wet, equatorial climate. The
impressively regular coastline runs north–south, constantly exposed
to the ocean swell. An inland waterway, the Canal des Pangalanes,
linking Toamasina and Manakara, has been restored to facilitate
commerce between the coastal towns. But canal is something of a
misnomer. It is more a chain of lagoons and vast lakes, watery
avenues and capricious channels, best suited to an outrigger canoe.
An occasional barge laden with graphite, or carrying a cargo of
sugar-cane or coffee, makes its ponderous way among the traditional Betsimisaraka craft. The original plan was to create a navi-
gable network extending 665 kilometres (415 miles) from
Foulpointe to Farafangana, but much work remains to be done.

*T*he *"pousse-pousse" is a picturesque means of transport, introduced by Pakistanis at the beginning of the century – an indicator of the island's low level of economic development.*

Near Ranohira, the mysterious sandstone massif of the Isalo has been eroded into all kinds of strange shapes.

From the jungle valleys of the Massif d'Ambre, which rises to 2,800 metres (9,100 ft) in the north of the island, to the semi-desert conditions of the vast Horombe Plateau in the south, Madagascar presents the visitor with one breathtaking landscape after another.

The Great Island's wealth of imposing natural features is a source of wonder and enchantment, which the incursions of tourism have done nothing to diminish. And the further south you travel, the stranger the landforms become.

First you must face the mists of the Ankaratra, the mountain range that forms the backbone of the island, and, further west, the mirage-inducing landscape of the Tampoketsa, an immense red plateau of eroded hills, where the earth, haunting in its sensuality, appears to languish under a burning fabric of blue fire. South of Ambalavao, the Andringitra range is formed of overlapping granite blocks dominated by the mass of Pic Boby (2,658 m/ 8,727 ft), Madagascar's second highest mountain, where the souls of the ancestors are said to hold council. As you come down out of the mountains, the Porte

du Sud, an immense cliff which glows red in the last rays of the sun, forms the gateway to Madagascar's Deep South, marking the frontier between the rounded green humps of the highlands and the immense Horombe Plateau stretching away below.

From this point on, there is a growing sense of penetrating into *terra incognita*: villages are few and far between, and the arid landscape opens up in cinemascopic grandeur. This is Bara country, a limitless prairie of yellowing grass dotted with satrana palms. Natural rebels, the powerfully built Bara are a race of pastoralists, some still living a nomadic life. They range the savannah with their herds of zebu, and occasionally engage in cattle rustling, an age-old tradition. From afar, the mysterious Isalo Massif breaks the monotony of the featureless plain: jagged crests, deep-carved canyons, eerie projections of worn, red sandstone – it looks more like a scene from the American West. These mountains are sacred to the Bara and, when venturing with a guide into this nature reserve, it is well to respect the established taboos (*fady*). The ancestors are said to have forbidden salt and the use of reeds.

*The baobab rarely grows beyond 25 m (82 ft),
but it can measure as much as 40 m (131 ft) in girth.*

• The baobab •

A large tree with a disproportionately thick trunk and tiny branches, the baobab can go on growing indefinitely. Despite its imposing mass, it is a fragile tree: its roots are tiny, and its wood yielding as butter if cut or stabbed with a knife. Though not suitable as timber, the baobab is of great value to the Malagasy. Its bark and leaves are used to prepare soothing infusions. Its leaves are dried in the shade and ground to produce a nutritious powder, which can be mixed with other foods. The tender green leaves are eaten as a vegetable. The dried pulp of its fruit, known as *pain de singe* (monkey bread), has a pleasant, slightly acid taste. In the west of Madagascar, baobabs are believed to have supernatural powers: evil spirits are held captive in their trunks and released to do mischief during the night. To protect themselves, the local people tie together three blades of grass growing at the foot of the tree.

*I*n the villages of the southwest,
around Tuléar, water is scarce and
the women often have to go long
distances in search of it. Over their
other clothes, they wear a brightly
coloured lamba.

Aloalo *are carved memorials marking Mahafaly tombs in the southwest of Madagascar. They depict the main events in the life of the deceased. They also form a link between heaven and earth. It is traditional to kill the cattle of the dead man and display their skulls on his tomb as evidence of his wealth.*

A land of rock and sand, the extreme south of Madagascar is home to the Mahafaly and Antandroy; two fiercely independent peoples who have adapted their way of life to the austere conditions of this desert of cactus, giant thorn bushes and succulent plants. ("Antandroy" in fact means "people of the thorns", the roy being a shrub with cruel spines.)

You need a 4x4 vehicle to visit this extraordinary region, and should camp among the tree-sized euphorbia and aloes to appreciate just how tough life can be. Dark skinned, distinctly African in physique, loud of speech and with a ready smile, the people of the south are warriors by temperament, as evidenced by the ever-present assegai. They surrendered only to the colonial troops of Colonel Lyautey at the turn of the century, provoking the remark from Captain Deefort that: "I can only compare the Antandroy, as a whole, to the stubborn Gauls described by Julius Caesar".

Living in small clans, subsisting on maize, millet, sweet potatoes, and Lima beans, rain permitting, they profess a boundless love for their cattle, prize freedom above all things, and take collective deci-

sions only after long, complicated discussions (*kabary*). Antandroy medicine men, who read the future with tamarind seeds and make healing ointments, are reputed throughout Madagascar for their knowledge of herbs. But so precarious are their circumstances that, in years of drought, the men are sometimes reduced to eating the boiled leaves of the prickly pear cactus (*raketa*).

Although the Mahafaly may spend his life in a tiny grass-thatched hut, he knows that, when he dies, his bones will rest in an enormous stone-built tomb, worthy of his entrance into the ranks of the ancestors. This tomb, or *valovato*, will reflect the wealth of the occupant, and is adorned with *aloalo*, wooden sculptures depicting scenes from his past life, and in some cases naive-style paintings. The more prosperous the dead man, and the more numerous his cattle, the more splendid his funeral celebrations will be. They include singing, dancing, drinking rum and firing shots into the air. But, above all, many head of cattle will be sacrificed, and their meat served to the assembled company. The skulls and horns are later arranged carefully around the tomb of their former owner.

A Malagasy warrior poses beside a Mahafaly tomb holding the giant egg of an aepyornis; an ostrich-like bird thought to have died out in the sixteenth century. Eggs are still sometimes found in the region of Amboasary.

*N*ine-tenths of the world's lemur species are native to Madagascar.

• Warning: species in danger •

A century ago, Madagascar was still the lemur paradise. Survivors of the Tertiary era, these primates, ancestors of the monkeys, are thought to have colonized the island, via Africa, some 40 million years ago. More than one early explorer is said to have trembled on hearing, from the depth of the forest, the roar of the ruffed lemur (*L. variagatus*). The most astonishing of all is the legendary aye-aye (*Daubentonia madagascariensis*), which was believed to have died out in the 1950s. Perching in the high fork of a tree, this ghost-like creature with the face of a medieval gargoyle, has an amazing middle finger; long and dry as a twig, which it uses for extracting grubs from their holes. But now it is under threat. Practising slash-and-burn methods, farmers have destroyed a good half of the forests. Although lemurs are regarded as taboo by many people, and therefore untouchable, their habitat seems likely to become more and more restricted.

Facing page: Pachypodium lamieri, *a bottle tree identified by its awesome array of triple spines.*

Madagascar has always fascinated botanists. As early as 1774, natural historian Philippe Commerson wrote: "There, nature seems to have withdrawn, as if into a private sanctuary, to work on models different from those She used elsewhere; there, you will find the most unusual, and wonderful, of natural forms".

The great rain forest of the eastern escarpment is a vestige of the island's original flora. All the tropical hardwoods so prized for timber – palisander, rosewood, mahogany and ebony – thrust upwards in their race for the sunlight. In the undergrowth, over a 100 species of orchid have been recorded, including the creamy white Sainte Marie comet, which has a corolla 38 cm (15 in) deep. Over 80 per cent of Madagascar's 12,000 species of flowering plant are in fact endemic, found nowhere else in the world.

But it is in the arid regions of the southwest, where plants have had to adapt to drought conditions, that they appear in all their extravagance. Is it that they are oriented towards the black continent? The bush of the west coast is certainly reminiscent of Africa, but in exaggerated form. Around Morondava, giant baobabs, which

This pitcher plant (Nepenthes madagascariensis), *which grows in the region of Fort-Dauphin, is carnivorous. Insects fall in and drown in its water-filled pitcher.*

can live for 2,000 years, rise in clumps from a soil tanned the colour of old leather. Madagascar has seven species; Africa only one. They are said to hold evil spirits captive in their trunks, and to release them at night. But do not worry: to ward them off, all you need do is tie together three blades of grass growing under the tree.

In the spiny forest of the extreme south, the brick-red landscape appears surreal in the rays of the setting sun. Candelabra-shaped euphorbia, tentacular octopus trees, tiny bottle baobabs swollen with water, bloated pachypodiums – also known as elephant's foot – fantsilohitras which extend their long scaly arms against the cobalt sky, enormous aloes, together form the backdrop to some extra-terrestrial fantasy.

The island's fauna is no less strange and archaic. Unlike Africa, Madagascar has no monkeys, big game species or elephants, but a host of primitive creatures, which come as a surprise. In the absence of major predators, and thanks to the dense forest which provided for their needs, many of the animals that had reached the island before it broke away from the African continent, 160 million years

ago, have been caught in a time warp. For instance, 30 species of that minuscule prehistoric monster – the chameleon – live in the forests of Madagascar. There are 3,000 kinds of butterfly, one more beautiful than another, including the charaxes, which are unique to the island. Sadly, only 300 or 400 specimens of the splendidly marked *angonaka*, or ploughshare tortoise (*Geochelone yniphora*), which lives in the region of Cap Saint André, now survive. Their numbers have been reduced by bush fires and wild boar, which are very partial to their eggs, and they have been taken by local people eager to make money out of their shells. As for the aepyornis, the giant ostrich-like bird which stood 3 metres (10 ft) tall and weighed 500 kilograms (1,100 pounds) – the "elephant bird" of Malagasy folklore – it is now the stuff of legend. According to Flacourt, it died out in the seventeenth century, but the Antandroy still occasionally find its eggs, buried in the sands of the south.

Madagascar is home to two-thirds of the world's known chameleon species. This is Chamaeleo parsoni. *The largest,* Chamaeleo ostaleti, *grows to 70 cm (27 in).*

At Tuléar (Toliary), fishermen use an ox cart to unload their catch.

*W*hen evening comes, the Vezo,
nomadic fishermen of the
southwest, use masts and sails
to pitch a tent for the night.

On the southwest coast, some 1,000 kilometres from Antananarivo, right on the Tropic of Capricorn, the Route Nationale 7 at last reaches its goal: the sun-drenched, dazzling white town of Tuléar. Wide avenues swelter in the heat, a burning wind scorches flame trees and tamarinds, the sun beats down overhead, and red dust blows in from the bush irritating the throat. The beauty of the south is harsh and violent. Tuléar awaits the cool of the evening to emerge from its lethargy. In the sandy lanes, the flickering light of paraffin lamps casts theatrical shadows. And in the discos, open to the ocean breeze, the music pulsates to an African rhythm.

The coastal villages on the edge of the semi-desert Mahafaly country are the territory of Vezo fishermen, who defy the ocean in flotillas of outrigger canoes. On Madagascar's west coast, the sea (*ranomasina* = salt water) breaks over coral reefs. Comb the beach and, half buried in the sand, worn, bleached, encrusted with barnacles and sometimes inhabited by hermit crabs, you will find specimens of tropical shellfish which are becoming all too rare: conchs, murex, giant clams, nautilus and cowries. With a little imagination, the driftwood might be taken

The church at Ambodifototra, on the east coast island of Sainte Marie, is the oldest in Madagascar. Its first bishop, Monseigneur Delmond, is buried there.

Simple though they may be, shops and small hotels in country areas are not devoid of charm.

for pirates' bones, long rolled on the bottom by the restless breakers. The coastline of Madagascar was for centuries the scene of buccaneering exploits, especially the delightful island of Sainte Marie, which lies off the east coast. As far back as 1685, this little paradise shaded by huge jackfruit trees became a strategic base for piracy, a safe distance from the petty kings of mainland Madagascar. Crumbling under a weight of luxuriant vegetation, epitaphs half eaten away by the tropical humidity, the cemetery where the pirates lie buried is still there, on Madame islet.

Sainte Marie – or Nosy Boraha, as it is now officially known – is a long tongue of land, lying parallel to the coast north of Mahavelona (Foulpointe). It has changed little over the intervening years. Life flows by, as the women plait one another's hair in the shade of the veranda, and the clove trees give off their pungent scent. Tracks disappear among the jambarakas, linking the tiny raised huts made of bamboo and thatched with the leaves of the traveller's palm. In the lagoon, women and children chant together as they close in on a shoal of fish they have encircled with their net.

And yet, the island has known some exciting times. All the best-known pirates hung out here at some time or another. Each gang imposed its own rules, forcing its members to swear an oath of allegiance on the crucifix, the Bible or an axe. In the eighteenth century, they eventually formed a tumultuous society, a 1,000 or more sailors of all nationalities, and got along well with the native population.

This fruitful cohabitation was to lead to a curious historical episode. The mulattos – descendants of these pirates and the daughters of local chiefs – soon established their hegemony over the entire east coast of Madagascar, as the apathetic Betsimisaraka tribes put up little resistance. One of these mulatto sovereigns, Queen Bety, married a French corporal, La Bigorne, who had fled to Madagascar to escape the anger of a jealous husband he had cuckolded back in the Ile Bourbon (now Réunion). This tropical Don Juan was so successful in arousing the francophile sentiments of Queen Bety that, in 1750, she granted Sainte Marie to the king of France. In fact, until quite recently, the people of the island were entitled to the status of citizens under French common law.

A banana leaf has many uses: as packaging material or as an umbrella.

Réunion stores huge reserves of water. From the Piton des Neiges (3,069 m / 10,080 ft) waterfalls, beloved of abseilers, spill down the sides of the mountain. Giant plant species, such as these tree ferns, flourish in the wet conditions.

According to the tourist brochures, Réunion is wild and secretive. More than that, the island is a hanging garden. Eight hundred kilometres (500 miles) from Madagascar, 200 kilometres (125 miles) from Mauritius, it emerged from a deep oceanic trench in recent geological time, forming two volcanoes with numerous craters. The landscape is mountainous. From the breakers which advance and withdraw over its coral reef to the Piton des Neiges, at 3,069 metres (10,080 ft), the terrain rises steeply, thrusting upwards. At midday, take the Route des Hauts, which winds up the mountainside through fields of sugar cane: the view down on the silvery mirror of the Indian Ocean, silent under the leaden weight of the sun, gives a sense of vertigo. "Three thousand metres (9,850 ft) under the water and 3,000 metres out of it, Réunion is like a big round egg. You feel lost in the immensity", the islanders will tell you.

But the time to see the volcano island in all its grandeur is at sunrise. You leave in the early hours from Saint Gilles, and take the road which climbs in tight hairpins through the geranium fields of the Petite France area, still hidden in mist, where intoxicating

gusts of perfume rise like the fragrance of the forest floor after a shower of rain. Traverse the virgin forest of tamarind and bamboo on the precipitous slopes of Piton Maïdo, then follow the footpath among the broom. Nothing can prepare you for the sight which suddenly appears. Opposite is the sheer drop of the Cirque de Mafate; at your feet a precipice: you are standing on the edge of an immense crater. It could almost be the first day of creation. The only sound is the yapping of dogs, somewhere below, in the depths of a valley. Below the rocky spurs which run out from the base of the cirque, still intersected by long shadows, the plateaux are coming to life; long stretches of bare country licked by powdery golden sunlight, showing between black ravines. The light is awe-inspiring, seeming to rise from the landscape like a cool breath. The only way to reach the houses whose corrugated iron roofs flash amid the dense vegetation is on foot, walking for hours on steep paths or by helicopter.

If you really want to experience light and shade on a grand scale, one day you should fly up through the Trou de Fer in a helicopter. The

*T*he Cirque de Mafate shows the
classic signs of erosion; at the foot of
the Crêtes de la Marianne runs the
Rivière des Galets. Despite the
altitude, it is warm enough to grow
bananas.

Weatherboarded houses are now a rare sight; corrugated iron has taken over. But the islanders have lost none of their fondness for vivid colours.

trip is only for those with a strong stomach. Playfully, the pilot flies low over the sugar-cane fields which rise from the coast, then suddenly, after crossing the crest of the cirque, everything falls away – 1,000 metres (3,300 ft) of emptiness below you, and the sheer cliff stretching endlessly away. The helicopter drops down into the shadows and follows a narrow, windy corridor, almost grazing the rock face with its profusion of lianas, tree ferns and chou-chou vines. Suddenly, you are flying into a funnel, with a waterfall ahead of you. The aircraft climbs again, waltzing slowly upwards towards the light, which appears to pour down through a hole into this green hell. The rest of the trip is equally fascinating. Seen from above, the cirques of Mafate, Salazie and Cilaos, arranged clover-like around the majestic Piton des Neiges, seem to have been slashed out by the billhook of some gigantic titan, creating deep gorges and narrow spurs, without any sense of restraint. In the south of the island, after flying over the monotonous expanses of reed-covered heathland known as the Plaine des Palmistes and the Plaine des Cafres, we approach a younger, active volcano, its presence announced by

a desert of ash. The Piton de la Fournaise appears at last, in all its mineral nudity, a strange lunar hump edged with precipices, its buboes of lava reeking of sulphur.

Rugged as the landscape of the cirques may be, even the deepest valley is inhabited. The P'tits Blancs who live way out in these remote *îlets* (hamlets) have chosen to turn their backs on the bustle of coastal life, even if it means being supplied from the air. Perched high up in their eyries for over a century, they belong body and soul to the mountains; like their ancestors, planters ruined by the early crises which hit the sugar industry. In common with the runaway slaves, they preferred a rough life in these remote highlands to employment on the larger plantations.

And all along these mountain tracks, nestling among mango trees and chou-chou vines, you come across Creole houses reflecting the mixed origins of the people of Réunion. The oldest – mere huts with shingle weatherboarding – were cut from the tamarind trees of these parts. Others, painted white or all colours of the rainbow, are reminiscent of the work of some naive artist, resplendent in their vivid hues.

*W*hen the volcano erupts, the Réunionnais rush out to watch,
hoping to see the molten lava clash with the incoming waves.

• The Piton de la Fournaise •

Still active, the Piton de la Fournaise (2,631 m / 8,640 ft), lording it over its immense outer crater, is a volcano of the Hawaiian type. It expresses itself in outpourings of liquid lava, which flow down as far as the coast. It can be reached by the road, from Saint Pierre and the Vingt Septième, crossing reed-covered heathland to the belvedere of the Nez du Boeuf, and on to the Enclos Fouqué, a hollow dotted with small black craters. The volcano erupts every ten months or so, but few of the lava flows extend beyond its immediate vicinity. In 1977, having for once overstepped its bounds, it was kind enough to spare the church of Sainte Rose, merely surrounding it with arms of red-hot lava. "La Fournaise is a well-mannered volcano", concedes Jean-Paul Toutain, responsible for the observatory on the Plaine des Cafres. In 1986, its lava flows added 25 hectares of land to the village of Saint Philippe. No doubt that is why the Réunionnais are fond of their volcano: every time it gets a bit overheated, their island grows a little in the immensity of the ocean.

An overseas *département* of France since 1946, the former Ile Bourbon (named in honour of the reigning dynasty) has plenty of surprises in store for *les zoreilles*, as visitors from Metropolitan France are known. As you drive along the coast road from Saint Denis to the lagoon resort of Saint Gilles, all the talk on the car radio is of traffic jams in Paris and how much snow has fallen in the Alps. You would hardly think that the "home country" was some 10,000 kilometres (6,250 miles) away!

In any case, the landscape is nothing like the stereotype of a tropical island. Where are the blue lagoons, the coconut palms swaying in the trade winds? Steep cliffs drop straight into the raging ocean, in a way more reminiscent of Brittany. To protect the corniche, the coastal strip is defended with 60,000 blocks of concrete, designed to break the force of the powerful waves which pour over onto the asphalt.

On the west coast, things are slightly different. Big hotel complexes, extravagantly lit up at night, have grown up along the road which runs between feathery *filaos* (casuarina trees), flanking the capricious

*F*ishing for zourites *(octopus) in*
the Étang Salé lagoon. A parasol is
an important accessory for women,
who do not like to get too tanned by
the sun.

lagoon of Saint Gilles. A paradise for surfers, windsurfers and big-game fishermen, these 30 kilometres (19 miles) of coastline, protected by a coral reef, are the only part of the island suited to conventional tourist activities. Réunion's champion surfers practise to their heart's content on the powerful rollers at Saint Leu, while others prefer to relax on the beach, cooled by a sea breeze. At the end of the last century, the children of the highland planters were already in the habit of coming down to picnic in this area with their *nénènes* (nannies), and to watch the crude rafts of the coral fishermen venture out into the foaming waves.

Farther south, around Étang Salé or Manapany, the ocean crashes into the jagged little inlets, throwing up geysers of spray from the basalt blow-holes. Here, many an unwary explorer has met an untimely end. Sheltered from the island's torrential rains, the leeward coast suffers from drought. The Saint Leu region is a land of goats, where weaver birds hang their nests on the skeletons of leafless palm trees: "Y resse pu qu'le balai, alors le coco lé arriéré, y donne pu!" (Only the broomstick is left; it doesn't give coconuts

In the Baie de Saint Paul, the only sheltered bay on the island, fishermen repair the nets they use for catching pêches cavales, *a kind of sardine which approaches the coast in shoals.*

Fishing in Réunion remains a small-scale activity, though efforts have been made to diversify and modernize the industry.

any more). The east coast, on the other hand, facing the wind, is very wet, clothed in great waving stands of bamboo.

Between these two extremities of drought and humidity, Réunion has no less than 120 microclimates. When it is "raining flour" (drizzling) at Saint Louis, there may be a steady downpour at Takamaka, which holds an impressive record for rainfall. Sometimes, the island laughs and cries at the same time, basking in sunlight as black storm clouds well up from nowhere.

From the water's edge to the mountain peaks or, to use the local expression, "des grand'cases du Bas aux paillotes des Hauts" (from the big houses of the lowlands to the straw huts of the highlands), almost all the population (half a million strong) speaks Creole. The language is the soil in which immigrants of very different origin have taken root over more than three centuries. Simplifying somewhat, it is usual to distinguish white Creoles (descendants of the wealthy planters), Cafres (of Malagasy or African origin), Malabars (Hindus), Zarabs (Indians of Muslim faith) and Chinese. There are very few who do not have a dark-skinned great-grand-

The local people are not put off by the unfavourable conditions of an inhospitable coastline. Fishing for shrimps (following pages) is a popular pastime.

mother somewhere back in their family history. Since settling in the eighteenth century to work the coffee, and later the sugar, plantations, they have learnt to love the beauties of their native island, without discrimination.

Just for fun, ask them to describe the typical Réunionnais: "Il a une chemise blanche et une bagnole devant la porte" (He wears a white shirt and has a car outside his house), some are bound to say. They will probably add that he tends to have a "tit nom gâté", like Titi Coco or Grand'Misère, a nickname which accompanies him throughout his life and even appears in the announcements of his death. Wives are stuck with the nickname of their husband: Mme Casse Couteau, Mme Coco l'Enfer and so on. Locals will also mention the *moukataz* – the art of making fun of yourself and others – which underlies every Creole conversation. But the first characteristic in most minds will be the strong tie which binds the islander to his island, his way of moulding himself to its contours, to the point of never saying "left or right", but always "up or down". Around the sugar refineries, great plumes of smoke belch out the

*T*he end of the nineteenth century
was a time of prosperity for the
Creole bourgeoisie, who built some
fine residences. These examples are
at Saint Denis.

sickly smell of spent cane. The traffic is slowed down by enormous *cachelots* (lorries) laden with newly cut cane, oozing sugary sap; more rarely by a team of oxen pulling one of the island's last remaining carts. In the misty canals, the *alizé* shakes the green canes of bamboo, which rustle like a dry waterfall. In the distance, at the end of its long avenue of cabbage trees, the plantation residence, dazzling white beneath the lacy shade of its fretwork, recalls the *dolce vita* enjoyed by settlers in the good old days – the "temps longtemps", as they say. Hidden away amid luxuriant vegetation, or sailing like opulent steamers on the silvery swell of the flowering sugar cane, there are still many of these Creole mansions on the windward side of the island. The diversity of their architecture comes as a surprise. Some, embellished with peristyles or antebellums in the neo-classical style, seem to have drawn their slightly sober inspiration from sixteenth-century Italy. Others betray the influence of distant Indian trading posts, boasting richly worked fanlights and delicately carved verandas. On the first plots of land granted by the Compagnie des Indes Orientales, the colonists were

With its lozenge motif and wooden fretwork, this Creole home is a place of great charm. Built of light timber, such houses are well suited to the tropical conditions.

at first content to erect simple frame dwellings made of ironwood and clad with tamarind weatherboarding. But as they grew more prosperous, towards the end of the eighteenth century, they built in stone or native timber, adding fretwork friezes of exquisite delicacy. And the townspeople of Saint Denis were not slow to imitate them. The Rue de Paris, the capital's main thoroughfare, is lined with a series of fine mansions. They can be glimpsed through gaps in their front gates, slumbering in the depths of their shady gardens amid mauve jacarandas.

Well ventilated by their many doors, which create welcome draughts, these cool dwellings are now feeling their age. The floors have been eaten by termites and, in the drawing rooms, patches of damp on the wallpaper attest to the damage caused by cyclones. But the art of gracious living has not changed. At midday, when the mountain outside is obscured by an incandescent haze, it is good to sit on the cool, well-aired veranda and enjoy a rum punch. In the demijohn, the home-made drink matures on its bed of lemon peel, vanilla, faham (a kind of orchid), aniseed and cinnamon. Seated in

Compagnie des Indes armchairs – made of Mauritius rosewood, palisander, fragrant camphor tree or some other precious hardwood – the guests linger. Creole hospitality has a ritual all its own. To get rid of an unwanted new arrival, the custom is to place an upturned slipper under his chair (it never fails!). But provided he has enjoyed your conversation, your host is bound to protest – in keeping with time-honoured tradition – "L'est encore bonne heure! Reste encore un peu!" (It is still early. Stay a bit longer).

The Maison du Général, a Creole mansion in the Rue de Paris at Saint Denis, once flanked by small huts.

Sugar cane remains the island's main agricultural resource. It is still cut by hand, as the rugged terrain does not lend itself to mechanization.

Réunion is not immune from the curse which afflicts all sugar-producing islands. Yet, supple as reed when cyclones strike, sugar cane remains the crop best suited to its rugged terrain. It covers 35,000 of the 53,000 hectares under cultivation. However, it accounts for only 30 per cent of the total value of agricultural production, a decrease from almost half in 1975. New crops introduced for the purposes of diversification – fruits, vegetables and flowers – have gradually caught up and overtaken it. The trouble is that sugar, sold to the European Union at three times the world price, is no longer a competitive option. It requires state subsidies, which may amount to 42 per cent of the total price. The plantation economy is slowly breaking down, and many of Réunion's 7,000 or 8,000 planters, particularly the smaller ones, are staring ruin in the face. Nowadays, only four sugar refineries are still operative, to the great displeasure of the local population. In the 1980s, when the Savannah refinery closed down, angry workers blocked the road, waving placards with the slogan "Préfet, casse pas nout bole de riz!" (Prefect, don't break our rice bowl).

*A*nthurium, *hibiscus and lilies
grow in profusion. In the area of the
"petite plaine", where there are
whole fields of them, the arum lilies
are picked in July.*

Réunion is an island of flowers. Their perfumes are everywhere: vanilla at Bras-Panon, vetiver at Le Tampon, rose geraniums in the Petite France area, mimosa on the Plaine des Cafres. It is a place of surprises: a little malabar shrine resplendent with marigolds appearing before you at a turn in the path; fire-walkers at a Tamil festival; or perhaps a Cafrine in a red dress and straw hat emerging from a cemetery under the frangipani trees, balancing on her head a woven basket full of grass for her goats. But it is in the island's mountains, when the sun has passed its zenith, that Réunion is at its most enchanting. At the heart of the Cirque de Salazie, Hell-bourg waits in a glorious haze. In the last, low rays of the setting sun, among the high mountains, the sugary perfume of the white and mauve-flowered francisea becomes overpowering. In planters made from hollowed-out tree trunks, maidenhair ferns open up in the moist evening air. And slowly, dusted with golden light, the planters' mansions sink into the dreamy shadowlands of their fragrant gardens.

Torrential downpours in the rainy season encourage the growth of dense vegetation.

*M*auritius has several Indian dance schools.
The richly adorned dancers wear the kanghivaram, *the most sumptuous of saris, the silk of which is interwoven with gold.*

Arab sailors called it Dinarobin; to the Portuguese, it was the Ilda do Cirné, Swan Island – a strange idea, since the only resident bird akin to the graceful swan was the comic, clumsy dodo, soon to be part of history! In 1598, the Dutch named the island Mauritius, in honour of their *stadhouter*, Maurice, Prince of Orange, Count of Nassau. They stayed long enough to ensure the extinction of the poor old dodo, clear the forests of ebony and tambalacoque, and introduce the tundjuc deer from Java. In 1715, the island became the Ile de France, under French suzerainty. This lasted until Nov. 29, 1810, when the British restored the name of Mauritius, which the islanders decided to retain after they had negotiated their independence in 1968. Perhaps we should add that the people of Réunion call it the "sister island", and it is acclaimed as the "Sugar Pearl of the Indian Ocean" – not bad for so small a dot of land! Just 63 kilometres (39 miles) by 46 (29), Mauritius is a tiny green emerald, set in the white swell that breaks over its coral reef, a spot of waving sugar cane in the immensity of the surrounding ocean. Mahé de la Bourdonnais foresaw that this island would become

*At Pamplemousses, in 1767, French intendant Pierre Poivre laid out the
Jardin Royal, planting large numbers of tropical species.
Giant water-lilies flourish in its magnificent ponds.*

• The botanical garden of Pamplemousses •

In the north of Mauritius, the garden as it stands today gives only a partial idea of its former splendour. Laid out in 1775 as a repository of tropical plant species, the arboretum was designed by the intendant-general, Pierre Poivre, as a garden fit for a king. Mauritius was then under the governorship of Mahé de la Bourdonnais, and the French dreamed of cultivating all kinds of spices and exotic plants for export to Europe. The work of tending the vast domain was entrusted to the botanist J. Nicolas de Céré. What now remains of this fabulous garden? Most famous perhaps are the talipot palms (*Corypha umbraculifera*) – strange trees which do not mature until the age of 60, then die immediately after flowering. At the end of a walk in the typically Creole style, which wends its way among lakes, stands of bamboo, and enclosures housing deer and tortoises, you come to the "Vallon", the rustic setting for Bernardin de Saint Pierre's romantic idyll of *Paul and Virginie*.

Mauritius has a thriving export business in model boats. Replicas of eighteenth- and nineteenth-century sailing vessels are the most sought after, but these local sailing boats are not without charm.

"the star and the key of the route to the Indies". Now experiencing an economic boom, like an intrepid southern Switzerland, Mauritius has proved him right. This speck of land, which trades with the Middle East, Indonesia, and Australia, while not forgetting its sentimental ties with Europe, has gradually entered into a multicultural, multilingual fourth dimension.

The variegated colours of Mauritius are a reminder of its cultural diversity. Its people hail from so many continents! It is not just the mynah bird and the canary that have adapted to its clear-watered lagoons. Take a look at the countryside. Observe the grace and radiance of the women in silken saris in even the poorest village; the roadside shrines to Siva and Kali; the Grand Bassin, whose waters are as sacred to Hindus as the Ganges itself; a village by the name of Benares; the Tamil Cavadee festivals, during which penitents fall into a trance and pierce tongue and face with long needles; the celebrations for Divali, festival of light. Might the observer not think he was in India? For here Indians are in the majority, accounting for 60 per cent of the population.

*P*icturesque salt pans in the
Tamarin region. It is the women
who harvest the salt.

Then there are the Creoles, of European, Malagasy or African ex-traction. To see them at their best, go to Chamaral on 15 August, to the fancy fair, to eat cari-singe and drink a few glasses of illicit tit lambik rum to the compelling rhythm of a sega. Someone takes up a *ravane*, the traditional goatskin tambourine, and they are away: up on their toes, breasts heaving in a sultry, erotic dance. And now-adays the traditional *maravanes* (rattles made with a tin box and beads) are supplemented by Western instruments (electric guitar, drums) and instruments of Indian origin (dholok, tablar, sitar). The Chinese, too, have their famous New Year festival. And the Muslims celebrate Yaum-Un-Nabi, the day of the prophet, and Eid-Ul-Fitr, marking the end of Ramadan. From the mosques comes the call of the muezzin, and the crowded booths of the bazaars have all the atmosphere of an oriental souk. Add to this colourful brew the fact that the Mauritians drive on the left (without much restraint!) and that the signposts are in English, though practically everyone understands and speaks the language of Bernardin de Saint Pierre, the French romantic writer, whose *Paul et Virginie* is set in the

*P*ort Louis, the capital of Mauritius, is built around the island's best-protected natural anchorage. It is a dynamic town, combining tradition and modernity.

Mauritian "Bois-Chéri" tea is renowned throughout the Indian Ocean. It is grown in the region of Curepipe, a town famed for its bronze statue of Paul and Virginie.

island, and you have some idea of this exuberant melting-pot. The local cuisine also reflects this diversity, embracing all five continents and coming up with some bold inventions of its own. Of course, you will find all the classics of Creole cookery: bouillon de bigorneaux (winkle soup), love-apple chutney, biriani with spices and aniseed, fried wasp grubs, or rougaille of dried octopus – island recipes with strong, unusual flavours. But in the bazaars, the cries of "Piments carry!" mix with the aromas of dholl puri, Indian lentil blinis, and the sales patter of the herbalists – an important facet of island life – talking up their traditional remedies.

From the interior of the island, there are views of the sea in every direction. Mauritius lost its mantle of forest long ago. The eye ranges far over the long waves of sugar cane; leaudiboute (l'eau debout = upright water) as it is called in one of the popular sirandes or Creole riddles. Here and there rise the sharp teeth of mountain peaks (known locally as *mornes*) said to have been sown by mythical giants: le Pouce, la Colline de Pailles, le Corps de Garde, les Trois Mamelles, le Mont Cocotte, les Montagnes Bambous:

Photographs of locals selling shells and coral will soon be a thing of the past. The government has banned the trade in order to preserve the fragile ecology of the island's coral plateaux.

names to savour, as if you were poring over a treasure map. But tourists tend to head for the 200 kilometres (125 miles) of coastline, with its string of highly individual coral beaches. In the south, the ocean swell, with a fury worthy of Brittany, beats against the volcanic basalt reefs of Gris-Gris and the Roche qui Pleure. In the wild hinterland, around the Morne Brabant, mongooses and macaque monkeys haunt the tall stands of timber, while tropic birds, trailing long white streamers, screech above the gorges of the Rivière Noire. The east coast, exposed to the trade winds, attracts only the most adventurous, despite the sumptuous beaches of Belle Mare and the Ile aux Cerfs. It is on the west and north coasts, with their deep, lazy lagoons and hotels of international standing, that the winter migrants of modern society – tourists hooked on the "big blue" – come to rest in the sand.

No less than in Réunion, the *varangue* is the key feature of the old planters' residences, which revel in such names as Eureka, Ville Bague, Château bel Ombre and Mon Plaisir. Built originally by ships' carpenters, these open verandas reflect a nautical way of life.

In the days of sailing ships, the roof of the *varangue*, or cockpit, under which the helmsman stood to work the wheel, was edged with a kind of fringe or lambrequin. It was in the time of Mahé de Labourdonnais and Pierre Poivre that stately residences of this kind were first erected on Mauritius. Whereas in Réunion they tended to be inspired by Palladian neo-classicism, on the Ile de France they borrowed more heavily from the baroque style of Pondicherry. These delightful houses with their graceful balustrades appear almost to float on air – an ideal setting for the quadrilles and mazurkas once performed on their waxed mahogany floors. It is a sad reflection that, in the towns, particularly the capital, Port Louis, these vestiges of the colonial past are now being sacrificed on the altar of urban development.

Well suited to the climate, the varangue *is the place to relax. It is a feature of the island's Creole residences, like the magnificent Château Labourdonnais (above), built in 1858. The house at the top of the page was built on Coco islet by a British governor in 1920.*

Driving in the Seychelles is quite an experience. On Mahé, the main island, the terrain is mountainous. With a sharp drop on one side, and no verges to speak of, the sinuous La Misère road climbs the mountainside in a series of hairpin bends, under a dense canopy of cinnamon trees. "It was built by a Môssieur Serpent", they will tell you. Turn off onto the Sans Souci road, and freewheel down between the red trunks of capucin trees. Below you, at the foot of precipitous cliffs, between tall stands of trees, the restless ocean is throwing up showers of spray.

Rugged geography is one of the first surprises the Seychelles hold in store. Grouped around the three main islands of Mahé, Praslin and La Digue, the archipelago consists of a hundred or so granitic and coralline islets, set in the intense blue ocean – a scattering of rocks and atolls left by the break-up of the mythical Gondwanaland. The most mysterious of all, Aldabra, a UNESCO world heritage site on a par with the Galapagos, is over 1,000 kilometres (625 miles) away. The elephantine rocks of La Digue, pink to the point of translucence at the Anse d'Argent, seem to stand guard on the

La Digue, with its chaos of granite rocks, has some of the Seychelles' finest beaches.

At present, you will not see many pleasure craft in the port of Mahé (the Seychelles' main island) because of the exorbitant harbour dues. The government has recently revised its policy and is encouraging yacht owners to visit the enchanting archipelago.

border of prehistoric times, an impression fostered by the sight of the inhabitants still living their lives to the slow rhythm of ox carts and bicycles.

Another surprise is the exotic-sounding place names, which merely reflect the presence of the French in the eighteenth century. The islands have charming, old-fashioned names such as Frégate, Silhouette, Denis, Cousin, Poivre, Félicité and Curieuse. The names of caravels, dukes and spices conserve the fragrance of the time when the early settlers cast anchor in these delightful bays and began planting the king's garden: 100 acres of vanilla, lemon grass, ylang-ylang, nutmeg, ginger or saffron to tickle the palate of the courtesans of Louis XV's court.

The shrewd Mahé de Labourdonnais, governor of the Ile de France (now Mauritius), had decided to explore the sea lanes to the north of Madagascar as a way of giving the English the slip. "We landed with our weapons to hand as usual, but found no one, and no sign of occupation", wrote Lazare Picault, captain of the *Tartane*, who had been sent to reconnoitre the newly sighted land. The date was

*S*norkelling *(without a harpoon) is popular on all the islands,*
but watch out for sea-urchins and stonefish.

• Underwater fauna •

The Seychelles harbour an immense wealth of spectacular sea creatures. The lagoons are enormous aquaria, inhabited by 900 or so species of fish, which exhibit a great diversity of extravagant forms. At Victoria (Mason's travel agency), semi-submersible, glass-bottomed boats can be hired to visit the Sainte Anne Marine National Park, opposite Mahé. You can take a magical excursion into gardens of island coral, observing vividly coloured zebra fish, the famous sergeant majors, moon fish, opulent damselfish, and shoals of curious parrot fish, which feed together on the growing branches of coral. Other denizens of these regions are the imperial angelfish, with their yellow, blue, green and black stripes, jacks, wahoos and the superb Picasso.

*B*ird Island and the Vallée de Mai on Praslin are like a lost Eden. A million-strong colony of sooty terns nests on the sands of Bird Island.

Though the island is only 1,500 m (roughly a mile) long, Bird Island Lodge has 25 tourist bungalows.

21 November 1742. And he was right. The Seychelles, which were named in honour of Moreau de Séchelle, Louis XV's controller-general of finances, had never before been trod by human foot. They remained French for 60 years, long enough to establish the colourful Creole mode of speech, which in the 1980s was declared the country's official language.

Since independence, achieved in 1976 after 160 years of British rule, the young republic has striven to preserve the wild beauty of the islands. The archipelago remains an unspoilt paradise, still faithful to the vision cherished by those who dream of remote Edens. Bird Island and Cousin Island (purchased in 1968 by the International Council for Bird Preservation) are sanctuaries for tens of thousands of nesting birds. Noddies, tropic birds, shear-waters, frigate birds, petrels and sandpipers can be observed from close quarters, going about their business without giving you a second thought. There is also the exquisite fairy tern.

As for the flora, the luxuriant forests are home to almost 75 endemic plant species. A striking example is the latanier palm,

which stands high on stilt-like roots. A stiff two-hour climb up the Morne de Copolia, on Mahé, brings you to granite outcrops where you can admire the rare, insect-eating pitcher plant. On Praslin, the Vallée de Mai, a 20-hectare nature reserve, leaves you with the slightly oppressive memory of a strange forest of half-dead, half-alive titans. The path winds its way beneath a tall, damp vault of cabbage trees and coco de mer – the famous *Lodoicea seychellarum*. Its ribbed leaves can grow up to 7 metres (23 ft), and many hang down, dry and broken, along the trunks of the trees. The coco de mer – the male bearing a phallic inflorescence covered with pungent-tasting yellow flowers; the female with its double-coconut fruit, for all the world like a woman's buttocks (hence the French term *coco-fesses*) – has always given rise to erotic legends. The local story is that they copulate at night, but you must not watch or you would lose your memory. The kernel of the nut is also supposed to have aphrodisiac properties, especially when mixed with calou, the local rum. The people of Praslin swear by it. No wonder Henri de Monfreid, in his day, described the Seychelles as the islands of love.

USEFUL INFORMATION

TOURIST INFORMATION: Maison du Tourisme de Madagascar, Place de l'Indépendance, BP 3224, Antananarivo 101; tel. 00261 2 32529, fax 00261 2 32537. There is no Malagasy tourist office in the UK.

LOCAL TOUR OPERATORS: CORTEZ EXPEDITIONS, 25, rue Zafindriandika, Antanimena, Antananarivo, tel. 00261 2 21974; MADAGASCAR AIRTOURS, 92, Hotel Hilton, Antananarivo, tel. 00261 2 341; VOYAGES BOURDON, 15, rue P. Lumumba, Antananarivo, tel. 00261 2 29696.

ENTRY REQUIREMENTS: A passport (valid for at least six months) and a visa are required.

MALAGASY CONSULATE IN LONDON: 16 Lanark Mansions, Pennard Road, London W12 8DT; tel. 0181 746 0133, fax 0181 746 0134.

VACCINATIONS AND HEALTH: Precautions against malaria, tetanus, and hepatitis (gamma-globulin) are not essential if you are arriving from Europe, but are nevertheless recommended. Check on the current situation with your doctor before you go. It is also advisable to take a few basic drugs and other medical items, as these are very difficult to obtain in Madagascar.

CURRENCY: The local currency is the Franc Malgache (FMG), with about 8,400 FMG to the pound (late 1997). Local currency may not be imported or exported, and foreign currency must be declared on arrival.

CUSTOMS: Strict import and export requirements apply to many types of goods, including tropical hardwoods and precious stones. If possible, get your customs and export forms filled in by your tour guide or by an authorized dealer.

Flights to Madagascar are operated by Air France and Air Madagascar. The journey from Europe takes about 11 hours non-stop, or up to 13 hours with stopovers.

THE COUNTRY AND ITS PEOPLE

GEOGRAPHY: Madagascar is located south of the equator, about 8,500 km (5,300 miles) from the UK. It is 1,580 km (990 miles) from north to south, and 580 km (360 miles) from west to east.

AREA: About 587,000 km^2 (227,000 square miles), roughly 2 ½ times the size of the UK.

CAPITAL: Antananarivo (Tananarive), population 1 million.

GOVERNMENT: Democratic republic. The President is Didier Ratsiraka, who was re-elected January 1997.

INDUSTRIES: The main industries are agriculture (with rice, vanilla, coffee and cloves as the main crops), tourism, and mining.

CLIMATE: The east coast is hot and wet; the west coast somewhat drier. The hot and rainy season lasts from November to April, while the weather is cooler from May to October. Temperatures in the highlands range from 10° to 25°C (50° to 77°F), while the coast is tropical. Many roads are impassable during the rainy season. Light cotton clothing is recommended throughout the year, together with a pullover and stout shoes.

LOCAL TIME: GMT + 3 hours.

POPULATION: 13 million. In addition to 18 Malayo-Indonesian ethnic groups, there are substantial Indian and Chinese minorities.

RELIGION: Over 50% of the population is Christian, though this does not necessarily preclude traditional animism and the cult of the ancestors, which are widely practised; there is also a small Muslim community.

LANGUAGE: The local language is Malagasy, with Merina being the official dialect. The other official language is French, which is spoken almost everywhere.

TOURIST ATTRACTIONS:

Madagascar needs to be tackled with a sense of adventure. Despite recent efforts, the country's tourism infrastructure is developing only slowly, and there is no question of touring the whole island in a few days. Apart from the new main arteries, the roads are often untarmacked and poorly maintained, and you should not expect sophisticated hotel facilities. But if you can adapt to its rhythm, the Red Island is a fascinating place to visit.

ANTANANARIVO, known as the city of a thousand colours, is the starting-point for most visitors to Madagascar and the base for many tours.

RÉSERVE DE BERENTY, a nature reserve with a great variety of native animals and plants.

NOSY BE, the "Fragrant Island", is the Tahiti of the Indian Ocean. It has a pleasant climate all the year round and a host of exotic plants and flowers, together with fine sand beaches and clear turquoise water.

NOSY KOMBA, the Island of the Lemurs. Can be combined with a visit to Nosy Tanikely, which is famous for its coral reefs and sandy beaches.

SAINTE MARIE (NOSY BORAHA), an island 60 km (37 miles) long, off the east coast of Madagascar, with luxuriant vegetation, unique orchids and wonderful opportunities for diving. From July to September, hundreds of hump-backed whales come here to calve.

USEFUL INFORMATION

TOURIST INFORMATION: French Tourist Office, 178 Piccadilly, London W1V 0AL; tel. 0171 493 6594, fax 0171 493 6594.

Comité du Tourisme de la Réunion, Résidence Vétiver, 23 rue Trouette, 97482 Saint Denis Cedex; tel. 00262 210041, fax 00262 202593.

ENTRY REQUIREMENTS: The same as for France; no visas are required by EU citizens.

VACCINATIONS AND HEALTH: Precautions against malaria and other diseases are not essential if you are arriving from Europe, but check on the current situation with your doctor before you go. Réunion's health system is of European standard.

CURRENCY: The local currency is the French franc (FRF), with about 9.8 FRF to the pound (late 1997).

FLIGHTS

Flights to Réunion are operated by Air France and Air Outre-Mer (AOM). The journey from Europe takes about 11 hours non-stop, or up to 15 hours with stopovers.

THE COUNTRY AND ITS PEOPLE

GEOGRAPHY: Réunion is one of the Mascarene Islands. It is located about 9,500 km (6,000 miles) from the UK, 1,700 km (1,100 miles) from Africa, and 800 km (500 miles) east of Madagascar. The island is 70 km (45 miles) from north to south, 50 km (30 miles) from west to east, has a coastline of around 200 km (125 miles), and is 2,512 km^2 (970 square miles) in area.

HIGHEST POINT: Pidon des Neiges, 3069 m (10,080 ft).

CAPITAL: Saint Denis (population 200,000).

GOVERNMENT: Réunion has been a French overseas department since 1946, and to all intents and purposes is an integral part of France.

INDUSTRIES: Sugar, vanilla, geranium perfumes and oils, fruit and flowers, tourism, manufacturing.

CLIMATE: Tropical, tempered by sea breezes and by altitude. The average daily temperature range on the coast is about 18° to 29°C (64° to 84°F), while the range in the highlands is about 5° to 18°C (41° to 64°F). There are two seasons: winter, from May to November, which is pleasantly warm, and summer, from December to April, which is hot and rainy. Cyclones sometimes occur between January and March. A jumper is recommended for higher altitudes.

LOCAL TIME: GMT + 4 hours.

POPULATION: 617,000. The largest ethnic group are Creoles, of mixed descent. Other groups include whites who have either migrated from France or were born on the island and are colloquially known as *z'oreilles*; Africans (known as *cafres*), Tamil Indians (*malabars*), Muslim Indians (*z'arabes*), and Chinese.

RELIGION: Most people are Catholics; there are also Muslim and Hindu minorities.

LANGUAGE: The official language is French; Creole, Chinese, and Indian languages are also spoken.

TOURIST ATTRACTIONS:
SAINT DENIS, the capital, with its market and elegant colonial buildings.
BOIS ROUGE and GRAND HAZIER in Sainte Suzanne: two beautiful Creole-style houses.
The MAISON DE LA VANILLE in Saint André: a chance to find out all about this fragrant plant (which is actually an orchid), and how it is used to make costly Bourbon vanilla.
SAINT PHILIPPE, with its fishing port and JARDIN DES PARFUMS ET DES ÉPICES.

The DESBASSAYNS FAMILY VILLA, now home to the MUSÉE VILLÈLE, which gives a glimpse of the great coffee and sugar plantations during their heyday. This beautiful mansion with its Doric columns was built in 1780, and still has the flat roof on which coffee beans were once dried.

STELLA MATUTINA, a museum chronicling the agricultural and industrial history of Réunion, and containing a wealth of information about the island's flourishing past and the role of the Compagnie des Indes.

The CONSERVATOIRE BOTANIQUE DE MASCARIN, at Les Colimaçons, which contains most of the plant species found on the island.

The CIMETIÈRE MARIN, beside the sea at Saint Paul. This is the final resting-place of the notorious pirate La Buse (The Buzzard), who was hanged in Saint Denis, and of the great poet Leconte de Lisle, who was born in Réunion.

The TROIS CIRQUES, a popular destination for trekkers:

- The CIRQUE DE CILAOS, surrounded by gravel deposits and reached via the village of the same name, which is famous for its thermal baths and fine lace embroidery. The area is ideal for walking, mountain climbing and white-water rafting.

- The CIRQUE DE SALAZIE, which is more verdant and has a number of waterfalls, best-known of which is the Cascade du Voile de la Mariée. From the top of the cirque there is a panoramic view of Hell-Bourg, a pretty village of Creole houses whose pleasantly cool climate makes it a popular destination in summer.

- The CIRQUE DE MAFATE and PITON MAIDO, a rugged and inaccessible region, home to some 600 people who live in isolated villages supplied by helicopter. You can also go hang-gliding here.

The PITON DE LA FOURNAISE, an active volcano set amid a lunar landscape of basalt rock formations. Helicopter flights give a bird's-eye view of this spectacular area.

USEFUL INFORMATION

TOURIST INFORMATION: Mauritius Tourism Promotion Authority London office: 32 Elvaston Place, London SW7; tel. 0171 584 3666, fax 0171 225 1135. Mauritius office: Emmanuel Anquetil Building, Sir Seewoosagur Ramgoolam Street, Port Louis; tel. 00230 2011703, fax 00230 2125142.

ENTRY REQUIREMENTS: A passport valid for at least six months is required, but visas are not necessary.

VACCINATIONS AND HEALTH: There are no compulsory vaccinations, and none of the serious diseases such as cholera and hepatitis found elsewhere in the tropics, though malaria sometimes occurs in the Port Louis area. Check on the current situation with your doctor before you go.

CURRENCY: The local currency is the Mauritian rupee (MUR or Rs.), with about Rs. 36 to the pound (late 1997).

FLIGHTS
Airlines operating flights to Mauritius include Air Mauritius, British Airways, Air France, Cathay Pacific, Singapore Airlines, and South African Airways. The journey from Europe takes 11 hours non-stop, or up to 15 hours with stopovers.

THE COUNTRY AND ITS PEOPLE

GEOGRAPHY: Mauritius is one of the Mascarene islands. It is located about 9,500 km (5,900 miles) from the UK, 1,100 km (700 miles) from Madagascar, and 180 km (110 miles) from Réunion. It is 65 km (40 miles) from north to south, 48 km (30 miles) from west to east, and 1,865 km^2 (727 square miles) in area.

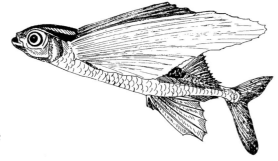

CAPITAL: Port Louis, population 150,000.

GOVERNMENT: Parliamentary republic since 1992.

INDUSTRIES: Sugar, tourism, tea. Mauritius is also a free-trade zone, which mainly affects the textile industry.

CLIMATE: Subtropical; sunny and warm all year round. The hot season lasts from November to March, when maximum temperatures range between 28° and 35°C

(82° and 95°F) and much of the rain falls in short, torrential showers. Cyclones sometimes occur from January to March. May to October is slightly cooler and drier, with maximum temperatures of between 22° and 25°C (72° and 77°F). July and August are windy on the east coast, and there are occasional showers.

LOCAL TIME: GMT + 4 hours.

POPULATION: Approximately 1 million, consisting of Indians, Europeans, Africans, and Chinese.

RELIGION: More than 50% of the people are Catholics; 25% are Muslims, and 18% Buddhists.

LANGUAGE: The official language is English; Creole, French, Chinese, and Indian languages are also spoken.

TOURIST ATTRACTIONS:

Both the coast and interior of Mauritius are very scenic. Some of the more attractive tourist destinations include the LAC DU GRAND BASSIN; the TERRES DE COULEURS DE CHARAMEL, an area famous for its multi-coloured soil; the botanical garden at Pamplemousses; the DOMAINE DU CHASSEUR, a huge forested estate which is ideal for walking; the aquarium; and the ÎLE AUX CERFS off the east coast.

USEFUL INFORMATION

TOURIST INFORMATION: Seychelles Tourist Office, 111 Baker Street, London
W1M 1FE; tel. 0171 224 1670, fax 0171 486 1352.
Tourist Information Office, Independence House, P.O. Box 92, Victoria,
Mahé, tel. 00248 229313, fax 00248 24035.

ENTRY REQUIREMENTS: A passport valid for at least six months is
required, but visas are not necessary. To receive a visitor's permit
on arrival, you must have booked accommodation, evidence of
having sufficient money to finance your stay, and a return air
ticket.

VACCINATIONS AND HEALTH: No vaccinations are essential if you are
arriving from Europe, and there are no serious tropical diseases
such as hepatitis and malaria. However, check on the current
situation with your doctor before you go.

CURRENCY: The local currency is the
Seychelles rupee (SCR or Rs.), with
about Rs. 8.4 to the pound (late 1997).

FLIGHTS
Flights to Mauritius are operated by Air Seychelles, Air France, British Airways and
Kenya Airways. The journey from Europe takes about 9 hours non-stop, or up to
16 hours with stopovers.

THE COUNTRY AND ITS PEOPLE

GEOGRAPHY: The Seychelles is a group of islands in the Indian Ocean. It consists of
four archipelagos totalling about 100 islands, and is located about 7,500 km (4,700
miles) from the UK and 1,600 km (1,000 miles) from the African coast. The
country is only 444 km^2 (173 square miles) in area, but spans around 400,000 km^2
(250,000 square miles) of ocean.

CAPITAL: Victoria, on the island of Mahé; population 30,000.

GOVERNMENT: Independent republic; the head of state is Albert René.

INDUSTRIES: Tourism, fishing, copra (dried coconut kernels), cinnamon, and guano.

CLIMATE: Tropical; hot all year round, with maximum temperatures ranging between 25° and 30°C (77° and 86°F). Short, heavy showers and thunderstorms are particularly common in December and January. As the climate is so hot, light cotton clothing is all you need.

LOCAL TIME: GMT + 4 hours.

POPULATION: Approximately 600,000, consisting mainly of Creoles, Indians, and Chinese.

RELIGION: 91% of the Seychellois are Catholics, and about 4% are Anglicans.

LANGUAGE: Most people speak Creole, though English and French are also official languages and are widely spoken.

TOURIST ATTRACTIONS:

THE INNER ISLANDS: Most of these are made of granite, rather than coral; the three main ones are MAHÉ, PRASLIN, and LA DIGUE. The latter is the most attractive, with superb beaches in the lee of granite cliffs; another is SILHOUETTE, which has no roads, primeval forests, and deserted beaches. DENIS has been called the pearl of the Indian Ocean, and boasts white sandy beaches and excellent fishing.

THE OUTER ISLANDS are all coral reefs with wonderful turquoise lagoons. Two of the most beautiful are BIRD, a nature reserve complete with millions of birds, and DESROCHES, one of the Amirantes group and a paradise for divers.

Although all information was carefully checked at the time of going to press (November 1997), the publisher cannot accept any responsibility for its accuracy.

Christian VAISSE: 12–13, 14, 15, 16 l, 17, 18–19, 20, 21, 24, 25, 26, 27, 28–29, 30, 31, 32, 33, 34–35, 36, 37, 38, 39, 40, 41, 44, 45, 46, 47, 48, 49 t, 49 br, 50, 52–53, 54, 55 t, 56, 57, 58–59, 60, 61, 62, 63, 64, 65, 66–67, 68 tbr, 69, 70, 71, 72, 73, 74–75, 76, 77, 78, 79, 80–81, 82, 83, 84, 85, 86, 87, 88–89, 90, 91, 92, 93, 94, 95, 98, 99, 100, 101, 103, 104–105, 106, 107, 108, 109, 110–111, 112, 113, 115, 116–117, 118, 119 b, 120–121, 122, 124 b, 126 br, 127, 128, 130 b, 132, 133, 135, 136–137, 143 t, 144, 145.

Christian BOSSUT-PICAT: 102, 146–147.

Gérard COULON: 22–23.

Maurice and Katia KRAFFT: 96, 97.

Claude PAVARD: 11, 42–43, 49 bl, 51, 55 b, 68 bl, 124 t, 131, 139, 142, 143 br, 143 bl.

Lionel POZZOLI: 140, 141.

Michel RENAUDEAU: 8–9, 123, 134, 138.

Guido Alberto ROSSI: 125.

Christophe VALENTIN: 119 t.

Emmanuel VALENTIN: 126 tbl, 129, 130 t.

Alfred WOLF: 16 r.

All the photographs are distributed by the Hoa-Qui Photographic Agency, Paris.
t: top; b: bottom; l: left; r: right